It's MY Body

by Lory Freeman
illustrations Carol Deach

Lory Freeman Britain, Ph.D. is program director for Relief Nursery, Inc. in Eugene, Oregon. She has extensive experience in early childhood education and sexual abuse prevention. Other books Dr. Britain has published with Parenting Press, Inc. are *Loving Touches* and *Mi Cuerpo Es MIO*, the Spanish translation of *It's MY Body*. She is the parent of two children.

Carol Deach is an award-winning artist from Washington State. Other Parenting Press, Inc. books illustrated by Ms. Deach include *Loving Touches, Mi Cuerpo Es Mio,* and *Something Happened and I'm Scared to Tell.* She is the parent of two children who sometimes model for her illustrations.

Parenting Press, Inc.
P.O. Box 75267
Seattle, Washington 98175
www.ParentingPress.com

INTRODUCTION

It is important for parents and teachers to foster independence in young children by teaching effective means for coping with various situations. Theories of child development emphasize achieving autonomy through increased initiative and a sense of mastery.

Dr. Lory Freeman Britain's book is consistent with these concepts, providing children an assertive stance for control of their own bodies and feelings. Her thoughtful approach prepares young children for appropriate responses to physical assault, and does so without provoking potentially damaging guilt feelings. *It's MY Body* is a sensitive way to introduce children to a prevalent problem in our culture.

Sondra Plone, Ph.D.
Los Angeles, California
October 1982

Dear Parents:

Until recently, sexual abuse was a crime rarely discussed with children. Most of us heard vague warnings about "strangers" from our parents, and we have, perhaps, relayed these warnings on to our children. However, few of us received any specific information about sexual abuse, or methods to use to protect ourselves. Thus, many conscientious parents hesitate to talk with their children about sexual abuse even though research has shown that children who have been informed about this crime are less likely to be victimized.

It's MY Body has been written in order to help adults and preschool children talk about sexual abuse together in a way which minimizes embarrassment and fear, but emphasizes self-reliance and open communication. You will not find specific references and stories about sexual abuse in this book. Preschool children are not ready for detailed discussions of this issue. They are ready, however, to learn how their feelings can help them make decisions about sharing their bodies, and how to communicate those decisions to others. This kind of learning serves as a vital first step in the protection of children from sexual abuse.

Thus we encourage you not to just read this book **to** your children, but to **share** the book together. As you read the text, ask your children to share their thoughts and feelings about different kinds of touch. Try to remember back to your childhood and recapture your childhood feelings about sharing your body. You may wish to tell your children about some of these experiences.

It's MY Body teaches children two "touching codes" which should become automatic responses to uncomfortable touch situations. This protective strategy for your children can be introduced by having them practice the codes with you as you read *It's MY Body*. Coach your children to look you in the eye, to hold up their hands, and to say the codes without giggling – like they "really mean it".

Once your children have learned these codes, you can reinforce their understanding by telling situation stories which involve the use of a touching code. For example, the touching code is an appropriate response to an unwanted hug, uncomfortable tickling or wrestling.

When you have finished reading *It's My Body* and talking about the touching codes, be sure to tell your children that if they are touched by anyone in a way that makes them feel uncomfortable, to come and tell you right away.

Most children like *IT'S MY Body* so much they want to hear it read over and over. This is well, as preventative safety teaching must be repeated often until children have truly absorbed the protective strategies.

It's MY Body provides parents with a positive, self-affirming method of protective teaching. We hope that you and your children will find sharing this book to be an enjoyable, growing experience.

Janie Hart-Rossi

Janie Hart-Rossi
Sexual Abuse Prevention Educator

I have something very special
that belongs to only me.

I was born with it . . .

And it changes as I grow older.

But it is always just mine!
It's my body.

Sometimes I like to share my body . . .

When I hug my father,
I am sharing my body.

When I sit on my grandma's lap,
I am sharing my body.

When I hold a little baby's hand,
I am sharing my body.

When I let someone tickle me,
I am sharing my body.

Even when I am sharing my body,
it is always something special that
belongs only to me.

Sometimes I don't like to share my body.

If someone is tickling me too hard,
I might not feel like sharing my body.

If someone wants to give me a big slurpy
kiss, I might not feel like sharing my body.

If a dog is licking me, I might not
want to share my body with the dog.

If someone is holding me too tightly,
I might not feel like sharing my body.

If someone wants to touch me any place
or way that makes me feel uncomfortable,
I won't share my body!

This is what I say:
"Don't touch me! I don't like it!"

If someone wants me to touch them
any place or way that makes me feel
uncomfortable, I won't share my body!

This is what I say:
"No, I won't touch you. I don't like it!"

Now YOU practice saying it loud and clear.
"Don't touch me! I don't like it!"

and . . .

"No, I won't touch you! I don't like it!"

You will probably feel warm inside when you share your body because you want to.

But, if you feel uncomfortable inside,
don't share your body!

Remember . . .
Your body is something very special
that belongs only to you!

More Books to Help Protect Children

It's My Body, by Lory Freeman and illustrated by Carol Deach, teaches children how to distinguish between "good" and "bad" touches, and how to respond appropriately to unwanted touches. Useful with 3-8 years, 32 pages, $7.95 paper, $16.95 library
Mi Cuerpo Es MIO, Spanish translation of *It's MY Body*. $7.95 paper
Protect Your Child from Sexual Abuse, by Janie Hart-Rossi offers parents information about sexual abuse and what to do to prevent child abuse. Useful with 1-12 years, 64 pages, $8.95 paper, $17.95 library
Loving Touches, by Lory Freeman and illustrated by Carol Deach, teaches children how to ask for and give positive and nurturing touches. Children also learn how to respect their own and other's bodies. Useful with 3-8 years, 32 pages, $7.95 paper, $16.95 library
Telling Isn't Tattling, by Kathryn Hammerseng and illustrated by Dave Garbot, helps children learn when to tell an adult they need help, and when to deal with problems themselves. Adults learn when to pay attention to kids' requests for help. Useful with 3-8 years, 32 pages, $7.95 paper, $16.95 library
The Trouble with Secrets, by Karen Johnsen and illustrated by Linda Johnson Forssell, shows children how to distinguish between hurtful secrets and good surprises. Useful with 3-8 years, 32 pages, $7.95 paper, $16.95 library
El Problema Con Los Secretos, Spanish translation of *The Trouble with Secrets*. $7.95 paper
Something Happened and I'm Scared to Tell, by Patricia Kehoe, Ph.D. and illustrated by Carol Deach, is the story of a young sexual abuse victim who learns how to recover self-esteem. Useful with 3-7 years, 32 pages, $7.95 paper, $16.95 library
Algo Pasó y Me Da Miedo Decirlo, Spanish translation of *Something Happened and I'm Scared to Tell*. $7.95 paper
Helping Abused Children, by Patricia Kehoe, Ph.D. provides many ideas and activities for care givers working with sexually abused children. Useful with 3-12 years, 48 pages, $10.95 paper, $18.95 library
Something Is Wrong at My House, by Diane Davis and illustrated by Marina Megale, offers children in violent homes ways to cope with the violence. Useful with 3-12 years, 40 pages, $7.95 paper, $16.95 library
Algo Anda Mal En Mi Casa, Spanish translation of *Something Is Wrong at My House*. $7.95 paper
Kids to the Rescue!, by Maribeth and Darwin Boelts and illustrated by Marina Megale, uses an interactive "what-would-you-do-if?" format, and prompts kids to think wisely in an emergency. Useful with 4-12 years, 72 pages, $8.95 paper, $18.95 library

---

Ask for these books at your favorite bookstore, call 1-800-992-6657, or visit us on the Internet at www.ParentingPress.com. Visa and MasterCard accepted. A complete catalog available upon request.

Parenting Press, Inc., P.O. Box 75267, Seattle, WA 98175

Prices subject to change without notice